BLESSED KATERI TEKAKWITHA
Mohawk Maiden

Blessed Kateri Tekakwitha

MOHAWK MAIDEN

By the Daughters of St. Paul

ST. PAUL EDITIONS

NIHIL OBSTAT:
Rev. Richard V. Lawlor, S.J.
Censor Deputatus

IMPRIMATUR:
+Humberto Cardinal Medeiros
Archbishop of Boston

ISBN   0-8198-1100-9 cloth
ISBN   0-8198-1101-7 paper

Printed in the U.S.A. by the Daughters of St. Paul
50 St. Paul's Ave., Boston, MA 02130

The Daughters of St. Paul are an international congregation of religious women serving the Church with the communications media.

Contents

Introduction

June 22, 1980, was a great day for North America. At St. Peter's Basilica, Rome, Pope John Paul II proclaimed that the "Lily of the Mohawks," Kateri Tekakwitha, shares in the eternal union with God enjoyed by the blessed.

Kateri was born in Ossernenon, now Auriesville, New York, in 1656, the daughter of a Mohawk chief and his Algonquin Christian squaw. After an obscure life of hardship and suffering, Kateri died at the early age of twenty-four. Today, three hundred years later, she is honored by hundreds of thousands of her brothers and sisters in Christ.

Kateri's life is an inspiration. Her world, like ours, was a changing one, in which the institutions of family and society were under constant threat. Kateri's response of faith in God and in Jesus' message of love points out the way for us.

She lived and died as a totally dedicated laywoman, sustained by prayer, loving kindness to others and adherence to moral values. How important are these same virtues for the rapidly changing period in which we live; may they lead us, as they led her, to grasp the true meaning of life—to find union with God.

Now, as then, the world needs young people who are ready and willing to accept the Gospel of Jesus Christ and give themselves in service to their fellow human beings. Now, as then, it cries out for youth who are courageous enough to pursue the vision of faith which inspired those who have gone before us.

Early Years

War cries and fierce drum beats filled the air. The Mohawk warriors had scored another victory. The peaceful Algonquin Indians had not been able to withstand their surprise attack. Many braves had been killed. Women and children were taken captives. They were rich prizes that could be kept or sold as slaves.

The warriors led their captives through forests and over lakes, along the war trail from the St. Lawrence River into the Valley of the Mohawks.

Kenhoronkwa, the Mohawk warrior chief, could not help but notice the gentleness and kindness of Kahenta, a young Algonquin maiden. He did not know that she was a Christian who had learned about the Great

Rawanniio[1] from the Blackrobes (Jesuit missionary priests).

Kenhoronkwa watched with both puzzlement and respect as Kahenta took on the heaviest burdens from the older women who easily grew tired on the fatiguing journey. This maiden was different from the others, and she was fast winning the chief's heart.

When they arrived at the Mohawk camp, Kenhoronkwa married Kahenta. Being the wife of a chief, she was treated well by the other Mohawks.

Kahenta soon adjusted to Mohawk living, and God blessed their marriage with a baby girl. She was her parents' delight.

Kenhoronkwa forgot all about his many worries, his war councils and his tribal meetings. He proudly held the infant in his arms and asked: "Kahenta, what shall we name our little one?"

Kahenta sighed. She wanted to give her child a Christian name, but she did not dare to suggest this to her husband.

"Let us call her Tekakwitha,"[2] she said.

1. *Rawanniio* was the Mohawk word for God.
2. According to Mohawk Indian custom a "baby name" was given the child at birth. Tekakwitha's "baby name" was *Ioragode* (Sunshine). She was actually called Tekakwitha when she was about four years old.

"That is a good name," agreed Kenhor-onkwa. "Tekakwitha will do just what her name means: she will *move-all-that-is-be-fore-her.*"

He then gently placed the sleeping child in her mother's arms and left.

Kahenta's eyes filled with tears. "Some-day," she said softly, "someday I will have the Blackrobes pour the water of life on you, my little one. Then you, too, will be a child of God."

"Hush! You must be careful of what you say," warned Anastasia, an older Christian squaw who loved Kahenta. "If you are not careful, our Great Chief will have all of us Christians punished."

Years passed and soon Tekakwitha was a lively child of four, following her mother everywhere, full of curiosity and always ask-ing questions. She loved to hear stories, especially those about Jesus, His Mother and the saints.

"Mamma, where do the birds come from?" asked Tekakwitha. She had heard the answer many times, but she liked to hear her mother repeat it again and again.

"God made them, my little one. God made all the beautiful things of this world: He made the trees, the flowers, the birds and the lakes; He made everything. Then He made Adam and Eve. They were our first parents.

"Because God loved Adam and Eve, He gave them each a soul which would live forever. That soul was made to God's image and likeness."

"I wish I could see the soul. It must be beautiful," said Tekakwitha.

"Yes, dear, and we must keep it beautiful by never committing any sins."

"Adam and Eve did."

"Yes, they disobeyed God and He punished them just as I punish you and your little brother when you misbehave. God sent them out of their beautiful garden, because by sinning they had lost sanctifying grace, God's special gift to man. But to show His love for our first parents and for us, He promised them a Redeemer, a Savior, who would come on earth, take away the sin from man and regain for him sanctifying grace. He would reopen the gates of heaven."

"Jesus opened heaven for us. And the beautiful Mary is His Mother and ours too!" cried Tekakwitha.

"Yes, my little one, and she loves us very much. Love her, and never offend her by sinning," said Kahenta.

Tekakwitha loved to hear stories, especially about Jesus and His Mother.

One day as she was walking with her mother, Tekakwitha heard strange drum beats.

"Mother, why are they beating the drums like that?" the frightened girl asked.

Kahenta put her arms around Tekakwitha and shook her head sadly.

"My little one, the *smallpox devil* has visited our tribe. Many of our dear friends have died already."

"What is the *smallpox devil*, Mother?"

"It is a sickness. When it strikes, it usually kills," answered Kahenta.

"But Father is a great chief. He will kill the *smallpox devil*," said Tekakwitha.

"My little one, it is not in his power. Only Rawanniio can help us."

While she was talking, Kahenta's arms let go of her child. Her eyes began to stare and she fell to the ground.

"Mother! Mother!" cried Tekakwitha. "Don't let the *smallpox devil* get you!"

But Kahenta did not hear. She was hot and feverish.

Anastasia came running as soon as she heard Tekakwitha scream. She tried to help Kahenta, but she could do nothing for her. The good squaw ran to see Tekakwitha's little brother. He lay so still on his mat....

Although she too contracted the dread disease, Tekakwitha survived the epidemic. Anastasia nursed the child back to health. Until the end of her life, however, Tekakwitha retained the marks of the illness: facial scars and partial blindness.

Hard Work

"Those couldn't be tears that I see? Not in the eyes of the Great Chief's daughter? Surely, I am mistaken!"

"Oh, Anastasia, why did you have to come in right now? I'm sorry, but I miss my parents and my little brother so very much. And now I have to leave you, too."

Tekakwitha fought hard to keep back new tears.

"My little one," Anastasia assured her, "we will still see each other often. And your Uncle Iowerano has the right to take you as his daughter. He loves you. You will be treated well. Iowerano is now the chief of the Turtle Clan and you must obey him."

"But his squaw doesn't smile. She doesn't like me," said Tekakwitha sadly.

"You're a good child. You'll obey Anastasia, won't you?"

"Yes, Anastasia, I'll try. But I wish I didn't have to go," insisted the little Indian girl. "I will never be able to become a Christian now."

Anastasia wrapped her big arms around Tekakwitha. "Don't worry," she said. "You will become a Christian and you will help many others become Christians, too!"

Tekakwitha's eyes opened wide. "Will I really? Then I will go to my uncle and be a good daughter!"

Soon Tekakwitha had learned many new skills. Chief Iowerano was proud of his niece. He had great plans for her future. True, her face was scarred and her eyesight poor, but her cheerful disposition seemed to make up for these handicaps. She was truly a chief's daughter.

But while Iowerano had words of praise for Tekakwitha,. his wife's jealousy led her to dislike the girl and place heavy demands on her.

One day Tekakwitha stole away to see Anastasia and opened up her heart to her:

"Oh, Anastasia, I miss you so much! My aunt never talks about God. She always scolds me when she sees me thinking. She says that I think too much."

"What do you mean, my child?" asked Anastasia.

"Well, sometimes when I'm alone, I think of the things you tell me."

"What, for example?"

"Well, I think of how good God is. He is our Father and watches over us. You said that He takes care of us and sends us rain when we need it. But when my aunt sees me thinking, she scolds me and makes me work."

"But you are only a child of nine."

"Yes, but she said that I must work and not be a lazy child."

"Tekakwitha, I think I hear your aunt calling you. Go quickly. I will speak to you again some other time."

Off Tekakwitha flew to her aunt.

"Where have you been?" asked Karitha.

"I went to visit Anastasia."

"Haven't I told you not to waste time? Come quickly. I will teach you how to clean the lodge. From now on you must do it yourself, do you understand?"

"Yes, Aunt," said little Tekakwitha, swallowing her tears.

The Indian maiden was now eleven years old. It did not seem possible that her small and slender body could stand the strain of so much work. But Tekakwitha had a strong will.

Because of her poor eyesight she always tried to stay indoors. Sunlight hurt her eyes.

One day, while she was busily making a new mat, Anastasia came to visit her. She appeared rather excited. What news could have made her so happy?

"Tekakwitha, the Blackrobes are coming! I heard them speaking with your uncle. They are to stay at *your uncle's lodge* for three days!"

"Anastasia!" exclaimed Tekakwitha happily.

"Your good mother's prayers will be answered. Perhaps you will receive Baptism soon."

"I hope so, Anastasia. I do want to become a child of God."

"Tekakwitha, Tekakwitha, where are you?" called Karitha. "Oh, there you are! Quickly: prepare the meal. We have guests. But don't you let me see you speak to them!"

Tekakwitha prepared for the guests. Then she went out to get some water. On her return she saw three Blackrobes who had come to speak to the Mohawk chiefs about a peace treaty with the French.

After the meal, Tekakwitha was busy cleaning the lodge as usual. One of the missionaries came up to her and asked: "Are you Tekakwitha?"

"Yes, I am," she answered.

"I am Father Pirron. Tell me, do you love Rawanniio as much as Anastasia said you do?"

"Oh, yes. I love Him and His Mother. I would be so happy if I could hear more about them."

"Well, pray to them and try to always be good and patient with all. You will be happy soon."

But Tekakwitha had to wait many years to be baptized.

"Tekakwitha," screamed Karitha one day, "come here at once! We must gather all our belongings. We are moving!"

Heavy packs on their backs, the Turtle Clan walked many miles through the forest. They halted on the north bank of the Mohawk River. This was to be their new home.

"Tekakwitha," called Karitha, "hurry! Don't be lazy! We must build our bark cabin quickly, because it might rain tonight."

The little Indian maiden never complained. She was very tired, but it was the women's duty to build their houses. The men only carried the heavy logs. The women did the rest.

"Anastasia," confided Tekakwitha that night, "I wish I could do something to show my love for God."

"Tekakwitha, my child, there is something you can do."

"What is it, Anastasia?"

"Instead of suffering everything in silence because you are the daughter of a chief, suffer it for the love of God. Make some sacrifices for the conversion of our people."

"Oh, yes, that I will do willingly. What else can I do?"

"Make acts of charity. For example, be as kind as you can to those who hurt you."

"Thank you, dear Anastasia, I will try my best to do so."

"Try to imitate the Blessed Virgin in her humility, modesty and charity, and you will be living a truly Christian life."

A Plan That Failed

"Your niece knows how to do many things," remarked one of the older Indian women. "The brave who marries her will be a lucky one!"

Iowerano nodded in agreement at the praise given to his niece. But he was not smiling. Tekakwitha was not like other girls her age. She kept apart and silent; very rarely was she seen at dances or village gatherings. Her aversion for Mohawk immorality and violence coupled to her love of seclusion strengthened in her the resolve not to marry.

More than once, Iowerano had tried to talk to her about marriage, but always her response was the same.

"Uncle, I love you as a father. You know that I have never disobeyed you. But I do *not* wish to marry! I beg you, let me keep my freedom!"

Neither Iowerano's pleas nor his threats could change her mind. Iowerano realized that this daughter of the Great Chief was not going to give in easily. And yet she *had* to marry, she *must*. Iowerano would not stand by idly while Tekakwitha brought disgrace to their family by her strange behavior. Together with his wife, Karitha, he contrived a clever trap for the Indian maiden.

"Tekakwitha," called Karitha, "tonight we are having special guests. You must dress in your finest robes and braid your hair with bright beads. A chief's daughter should look her best when guests are present."

The "guests" turned out to be the family of a handsome Mohawk brave. As he greeted Iowerano, he presented him with an expensive gift of furs. The two men exchanged smiles and nods—all of which escaped Tekakwitha's notice.

Everyone was seated for the evening meal. Talking and laughter filled the longhouse. At the height of the merriment, Karitha brought a bowl of cornmeal to Tekakwitha.

"All right, you may have won this time," he declared, "but I will not put up with your foolish behavior again."

Motioning to the young brave, Karitha said, "Here, offer this to our guest."

Tekakwitha lifted the bowl and stretched out her arms to offer it to him. The lodge became strangely quiet. Suddenly Tekakwitha's heart stood still. Everyone was looking at her.

Then, as if a voice within her had spoken a warning, everything became clear. These guests had come to a marriage ceremony. It was the custom among the Mohawks for the brave's family to come to the longhouse where the maiden lived. They brought gifts to the father. Then, when everyone was seated, the Mohawk girl offered a bowl of cornmeal to the young brave. When he accepted it, the simple ceremony was over. The two were married.

The smiling brave waited for Tekakwitha to hand him the cornmeal. Instead, she threw down the bowl and ran out into the dark night. Iowerano ran after her.

The shocked guests stood up angrily.

"What an insult!"

"What's the matter with the girl?!"

"Any young maiden would be fortunate to marry such a fine brave."

Horrified, Karitha tried to calm down the rejected suitor and his family. She knew that such an incident could easily dishonor their family's name.

"She's very shy. I'm sure she did not mean to insult him. Iowerano will bring her back. Please sit down and finish eating."

Hours went by and neither Tekakwitha nor Iowerano returned. The offended guests left. It was obvious to them that the plan had failed.

Karitha was still raging with anger when Iowerano finally returned home alone. "That stupid girl! How will we ever find someone to marry her now?!" she sputtered.

Iowerano saved his fury for the next morning when Tekakwitha returned home after spending the entire night hiding in the forest.

"All right, you may have won this time," he declared, "but I will not put up with your foolish behavior again. Perhaps hard work will bring you to your senses."

From that time on, Tekakwitha was treated like a slave and given the hardest chores to do. She had to gather firewood in the bitter cold of winter. More than once, her fingers almost froze.

Long hours were spent in the cornfields. The bright sunlight brought constant irritation to her weak eyes.

But worse suffering came each time Iowerano tried to force her into marriage. Again and again she rejected the warriors that came to claim her. She fled into the woods at the slightest hint of preparations for a new "marriage trap." And after each flight, she returned to face a furious aunt and uncle whose punishments grew ever more severe.

But Tekakwitha did not mind the harsh treatment. She did all that was asked of her and more. Often she visited the sick and poor of the village, helping them in whatever way possible.

Her goodness was rewarded. The Black-robes came to her village. Tekakwitha waited for the chance to speak to them alone.

Often she visited the sick and poor of the village, helping them in whatever way possible.

A New Life Begins

It was a bright June day. Together with several men, Tekakwitha's uncle had gone hunting.

Her aunt was with the other women in the cornfields and gardens. No rain had fallen for two weeks so the women and children had gone to carry buckets of water from the river to the dry plants. The village was quiet. Its only inhabitants were the sick and elderly who sat in the shade of their longhouses.

Father de Lamberville took this occasion to visit the various lodges.

At noon he came to the lodge of Iowerano. Into this house he was never admitted. The house seemed empty, and so, with a prayer in his heart for the unfriendly chief, he started walking past the door.

A voice from the corner of the house called out to him, "Father! Father!"

"Yes, who is calling me? Oh, there you are. How may I help you? ...I see you have injured your leg. Does it hurt you?"

Tekakwitha's serious eyes looked up at the gentle face of the Blackrobe.

"I cut my leg while I was hoeing in the cornfields, but it isn't my leg that's bothering me. Father, I have been afraid to speak with you but I can no longer hold back the desire of my heart. Please, may I be baptized? I want to belong completely to Rawanniio."

The priest had not expected the sudden, heartfelt plea. For a few moments he remained silent and pensive. Then he said, "My child, I believe that your intention comes from an honest heart. But it will require much strength of will. What led you to this decision?"

Tekakwitha told him of her mother who had been a fervent Christian, and of Anastasia, her mother's friend.

She described the desire she had felt from childhood on, to belong to the true God, to be a Christian.

"Tekakwitha," asked Father de Lamberville, "what if your uncle should forbid you to become a Christian, would you still go ahead against his will and remain firm in your decision?"

"Father, this decision must be my own. Surely my uncle will try to hinder me and he might even punish me, but Rawanniio will help me to be strong."

Tekakwitha waited for the right moment to present the question of Baptism to her uncle.

It came a few weeks later, when Iowerano returned home after a successful hunt. Once the evening meal was finished, he contentedly smoked his pipe and told the story of how he had skillfully outwitted the deer that was now proudly displayed outside his lodge. The Indian children who had gathered around the fire were wide-eyed as Iowerano supplied them with each suspense-filled detail. The chief enjoyed being the center of attention, yet he noticed that his story had not captured everyone.

"Tekakwitha," he asked, with a note of mock injury in his voice, "doesn't my story interest you? Your thoughts seem to be far away tonight. Don't tell me that you've finally fallen in love with a handsome brave?"

His comments brought laughter from the others. Tekakwitha smiled, but her cheeks flushed at his words.

"No, Uncle, it is not a brave that is on my mind. But there is something I would like to talk to you about."

Iowerano looked at his niece. Even when she was happy and smiling, her eyes maintained a certain serious expression. With a sigh, he had to again admit to himself that this girl was not like the others in the village. What thoughts were on her mind now?

"Speak, my niece, I will listen to your words."

"Uncle, I wish to be baptized by the Blackrobes. I want to be a Christian. The Rawanniio of the Blackrobes is the one, true God and He is the God I wish to follow."

Shrieks of horror and words of protest were heard around the fire. Then all silently waited for Chief Iowerano to speak. How would he answer this insane request?

Iowerano's first urge was to let his full fury loose on Tekakwitha. But was this the best way to change this stubborn girl's mind? He had lashed out against her with threats and punishments when she refused to marry and it had only increased her determination to resist. She had a fearless, iron will—so characteristic of a true Mohawk! If he openly opposed this new idea, she might even run away

Iowerano's first urge was to let his full fury loose on Tekakwitha.

to join another village where Christian converts were found in larger numbers.

The murmuring had started up again. Everyone wondered why the chief was taking so long to answer Tekakwitha.

"Silence," roared Iowerano, "I will handle this matter as *I* see fit. And you, foolish girl—I will speak with you tomorrow!"

But the next day, Iowerano did not bring up the subject of Tekakwitha's Baptism. Nor did he in the days that followed. The Indian maiden took his silence to be a form of consent. Under the guidance and direction of Father de Lamberville, she began the long period of study needed for converts.

The missionary was astonished at the clarity and depth of her insights. Whenever she did not fully understand a point of doctrine, she would simply ask for further explanation. Hers was a docile spirit, open to the light of truth and grace, thirsty for the waters of eternal life.

Usually those taking instruction found difficulty not in the truths of Faith, but in the day-to-day living of a truly Christian life. Christian virtues were entirely divorced from the pagan mentality that surrounded them. But Father de Lamberville soon realized that Tekakwitha was a shining exception to this rule. As a child, she had received both simple instruction and example from her mother. This basic foundation of moral goodness had fostered the growth of the natural law of right and wrong within her. Indeed, the Christians of her village assured the priest that she had always lived apart from the sinful habits of her pagan neighbors. Father de Lamberville's doubts were resolved and he decided the young Indian girl could be baptized.

On Easter Sunday, April 18, 1676 (Tekak-witha's twentieth birthday), she heard the beautiful words, "Kateri, I baptize you in the name of the Father and of the Son and of the Holy Spirit."

It was the dawn of a new life, the rising of a brilliant light on the North American continent. And the rays of this light would transform the darkness around and penetrate eternity itself.

"Kateri, I baptize you in the name of the Father and of the Son and of the Holy Spirit."

Trials and Escape

The desire that had been Kateri's for so long was now a reality. The joy and peace of her soul was obvious in the radiant smile that gave her scarred face a glow of beauty. She was now a Christian, and the happiness that came from this one simple thought could not be taken from her.

Trials and sufferings were soon to come her way. Iowerano's and Karitha's silence did not represent a sudden change of heart. They had not openly opposed her because they knew this would only further her resolve. But they did have a plan for bringing this "foolish Christian girl" to her senses. It would be a battle of wits and they were confident of winning!

Kateri attended Mass every Sunday. She tried her best to keep God's commandments.

One Sunday when Kateri returned from Mass, Karitha met her at the doorway.

"You're late for work. Hurry and eat breakfast, then come to the cornfield. Our plants need watering."

"But, Aunt, it is Sunday. You know that I am not allowed to work in the fields today. It would be against the commandment of Ra-wanniio."

"That's a clever excuse of the lazy Christians. If you refuse to work, all right. But neither shall you eat! After you've fasted the whole day, I am sure you'll be willing to work next Sunday."

Kateri remained determined. For the next few months she had to spend Sundays without a meal. She was forbidden to cook any food and was not given a share of the dinner which her aunt prepared after work in the evening.

While her aunt enjoyed an abundant meal with Iowerano, Kateri squatted at her bedside, weak and dizzy from hunger. A handful of dry maize was all she had had the whole day. She did not waver, though, but remained steadfast, friendly and obedient, although every Sunday brought a renewal of suffering.

But this was just one of the many trials Kateri had to endure. The children were encouraged to throw stones at her and shout insulting taunts whenever she passed by. They called her "the Christian" and "the sorceress" in the same deriding tone of voice.

And to these pains was added the still greater pain of loneliness. Her Christian friend, Anastasia, had gone to Canada to join a Christian village which the Blackrobes had started for Indian converts. Kateri missed her and begged her uncle for permission to go and live with Anastasia. But Iowerano refused to let her go.

Despite these trials, Kateri remained strong and firm in her new Faith. She often repeated to those who tried to lure her away from its dedicated practice that she would rather die than renounce her Faith.

Her chance to prove this statement true came one day when she was alone in her cabin.

A Mohawk warrior, whose love for Kateri had been frustrated by her refusal to marry, rushed in upon her without any warning. His eyes raged with the passion of one intent on having his way. Kateri rejected his rough advances. In a final attempt to have her, he raised his hatchet as if to strike her at any moment. Kateri's only response was to fall to her knees, quietly praying with her whole heart and soul. Her action brought total dismay to the warrior. The hatchet fell from his hand as he stood in shame at his own weakness compared to this woman's strength.

.The months of suffering continued. Then one day, new hope came into Kateri's life. An Oneida chief, Louis, who had become a Christian, and a Huron companion were preaching among the tribes in the Mohawk valley.

Kateri knew that this was the chance she had long been awaiting. She approached the two Indian missionaries.

"Please take me to Canada when you leave! I want to live where I can practice my religion freely with my Christian brothers!"

"We will gladly take you," Louis said, "but do you have permission to come?"

"No, I don't. And I know that my uncle would never give me permission, although my aunt would be happy to see me go. Please take me!"

The two missionaries agreed to take Kateri back with them. Together with Father

In a final attempt to have her, he raised his hatchet....

de Lamberville, they carefully planned her escape. They would have to wait for just the right moment.

Father de Lamberville learned that Iowerano was away at the trading post. He quickly informed the two men and sent for Kateri.

"Kateri," explained Father de Lamberville, "tonight when you are sure everyone is asleep, you must slip away into the woods. Louis and the Huron will be waiting for you there."

That night Kateri lay motionless on her mat. She listened carefully until the steady breathing of those around her assured her that they were sound asleep. Silently she picked up her small bundle and crept out of the longhouse.

Her absence was not discovered until the next morning. Karitha flew into a rage, immediately sending the fastest messenger to bring the bad news to Iowerano.

The chief was furious and set out at once to find the fugitive. But he was unable to overtake his niece and her companions. He returned home, admitting defeat.

**Silently she picked up her small
bundle and crept out of the
longhouse.**

A Special Christmas

Three weeks later, after a long, arduous journey, Kateri arrived at Caughnawaga, a settlement on the banks of the St. Lawrence River, not far from Montreal. The aged Anastasia was there to greet her. Kateri was overjoyed when she learned that she would be living in the same cabin as Anastasia.

"Oh, Anastasia, how happy I am! My soul is like a bird that has found its nest."

"Come," said Anastasia, "let us go to thank Rawanniio for the many blessings He has given us."

Tears filled Kateri's eyes when she saw the small mission chapel. It was the first time she had ever seen a church.

"Oh, Anastasia.... My soul is like a bird that has found its nest."

She knelt down to pray, as she had so many times before on the forest ground. "Jesus, how happy I am to be close to You. Now I can attend Mass every day.

"Oh, if only I could receive You in Holy Communion. How my heart desires this meeting with You. Let it be soon, Lord, let it be soon."

Father Cholenec prepared the newly-baptized Christians for their first Holy Communion. Daily Kateri attended his classes, seeking to further her understanding of this great mystery of faith. Father Cholenec could not help but notice how attentively she listened to his every word. Nor did Kateri's many acts of charity escape him. In simplicity and silence she nursed the sick, cared for the children, and reached out to help her neighbor in whatever way she could.

The Jesuit missionary knew that new converts had to wait at least a year before receiving their first Communion. But he felt an exception should be made for Kateri. As he explained to Father Fremin, the superior of the mission, "Kateri is so well disposed and desires to receive our Lord with such great eagerness, that it would not be right to deprive her of this grace."

Father Fremin agreed wholeheartedly. "Tell her that she can receive her first Communion on Christmas day."

"Kateri, let me help you get ready. Here is a new dress and some wampum beads. You must look your very best for your first meeting with Jesus."

"But, Anastasia, Jesus does not look for external decorations; He looks at the heart."

"Yes, yes," agreed Anastasia, "but still you must look nice.... At least wear some of the beads."

"Anastasia," Kateri replied in a soft but sure voice, "on the cross Jesus did not wear fine clothes. His was a pure, simple love of total giving and that is the love I wish to return to Him."

Anastasia was without words. She silently put the beads away and let Kateri attend Christmas Mass in a plain, unadorned garment, wearing only her rosary beads around her neck.

The entire Christian community celebrated the coming of the Christ Child into the world and Kateri celebrated His coming into her heart. Long after everyone else had left the church, she remained alone thanking Jesus for that precious moment.

And this first fervor did not die. The women vied with one another to be near Kateri during Mass, because just the sight of her helped them to prepare to receive Holy Communion more reverently.

Indeed, as Father Cholenec recorded in his diary, "From that day on, Kateri appeared different to us because she remained so full of God and of love for Him."

**The entire Christian community
celebrated the coming of the Christ
Child into the world and Kateri
celebrated His coming into her heart.**

A Painful
Misunderstanding

"Oh, look, Anastasia, it's snowing. I hope it will not be a heavy snowfall; we are to leave for the 'great hunt' in a few days."

Anastasia smiled at Kateri's anxious comments on the weather conditions. It was obvious that her excitement was mounting as the day for the hunt's departure drew near. It was no wonder, for the winter hunt was an ancient custom of the Mohawks. Each year at the end of December, the families of Caughnawaga would leave their settlement in small groups to stalk fresh game in the forests near the Ottawa River or in the mountain region of the Adirondacks. The hunt usually lasted for about three months. Temporary lodges were erected which housed the Indians during this time.

Kateri enjoyed this long stay, and looked forward to it. This particular year, though, the "great hunt" brought Kateri much sorrow.

An unfortunate and painful misunderstanding took place toward the end of the winter hunt which caused Kateri much anguish of mind and soul. The main figures in the incident were Nemahbin, a pious and devout woman except for her strong tendency toward jealousy, and her husband, Onsigongo. The couple had been happily married for twenty years. Onsigongo had never given his wife any reason for complaint, yet she carefully watched him, because his pleasant disposition made him a popular person in the community.

Nemahbin felt that her husband was too friendly with the younger women in the camp. Actually, he was equally friendly with everyone—men, women and children.

One evening he returned home very tired and sat down in the first empty place he found, which happened to be next to Kateri. He soon made one of his humorous remarks which caused her to chuckle.

His wife was sitting at the other end of the lodge. She observed the two together but could not hear what was being said. Immediately she began to wonder.

Her suspicion increased when she noticed that during the daily afternoon period of rest, Kateri would quietly slip away for the entire hour. Perhaps the two of them were meeting secretly in the forest?

Not wishing to jump to a conclusion without further evidence, she waited and watched for further proof which would confirm her thoughts. The "proof" came a few days later.

Onsigongo came into the cabin where the women were working on their handicrafts. As usual, he smiled broadly.

"My new canoe is finally finished," he happily announced. "Only the seams remain to be stitched.... Kateri, you're known for your skillful stitching. Will you do it for me?"

Responding with the generosity that was so typical of her, Kateri immediately got up to get her sewing kit and left with Onsigongo.

The simple conversation and Kateri's quick response did not escape Nemahbin's watchful eye. She was now fully convinced that the two of them were too friendly toward each other. Tomorrow they would be back at the Christian settlement. She would present the entire matter to Father Cholenec and urge

him to have a serious talk with Kateri about
the danger of being too friendly with a married man.

Meanwhile, she confided her story to Anastasia, who at first was greatly disturbed and
bewildered; but she quickly realized that Kateri would never willingly consent to anything
she knew was wrong. Still, she felt that Kateri could use some instruction on the subject.

"Kateri, a young woman your age must
be extremely prudent at all times. Especially
with married men you must be careful to keep
your place and never speak or meet with them
in quiet places."

Kateri listened attentively to Anastasia's
words. She was a bit puzzled by the sudden
sermon on a topic that did not seem to apply
to her. But she gratefully accepted the advice.

The next morning, Father Cholenec called
Kateri aside after Mass.

He spoke in general terms on the same
subject about which Anastasia had spoken the
day before. Kateri did not understand why
such stern sermons were being addressed
to her.

As he spoke, Father Cholenec studied her
face, watching to see if his words would cause
a reaction that would prove or disprove the
accusation. But all that could be seen was the

usual innocence and sincerity which charac-
teristically reflected the inner peace and joy
that was Kateri's. She was politely listening to
his every word but there was not the slightest
indication that his words were being heard by
one who was in personal need of them.

Perhaps he was not being specific
enough. He had never doubted Kateri's virtue, yet the woman who had brought the
charges to his attention was also known for
her virtue. He had to be certain.

"Kateri, there are a few questions I must
ask you. I beg you to answer them in all
truth."

Kateri noticed the serious tone of his
voice. "Yes, Father, of course."

"During your stay at the winter camp,
did you go in the forest alone each day? And
did you do so secretly, hoping no one would
notice you?"

Kateri answered with a simple, "Yes."

Father Cholenec continued, "Did you
meet someone in the forest and talk to him?"

Kateri's cheeks reddened at Father's
words, but she remained calm. Now she understood why Anastasia and Father Cholenec
had spoken to her so sternly.

"Yes, Father, I spoke to someone, but it
was not a man. I went each day to pray to

"Kateri, there are a few questions I must ask you. I beg you to answer them in all truth."

Jesus. My soul felt the need to spend that hour with Him each day. I wish to keep this a secret, so please do not tell the other women. It does not matter if they suspect me of evil. My soul must answer to God alone."

Kateri's words and the serenity with which she had expressed them convinced Father Cholenec of her innocence. The next day he went to see Nemahbin, and he assured her that after a thorough investigation, he had found her suspicions to be completely groundless.

But the shadow of doubt remained with Nemahbin and with the other squaws who had heard the story. They continued to keep a careful eye on Kateri, lest any new clues reveal themselves.

Their looks did not escape Kateri. They were a cause of deep suffering for her, but such suffering was willingly and cheerfully borne for love of the crucified Jesus.

In time, the squaws realized that their "watch" was serving to further prove Kateri's unblemished virtue.

A Holy Friendship

Kateri stood looking up at the large wooden cross that had been hoisted into place earlier that day. The new chapel was almost completed. She could hear the workmen's rhythmic hammering, pounding the last nails into place.

She walked around to inspect the side of the chapel. To her surprise, she found another squaw there, Marie Theresa. Kateri had heard of her but never met her until now. They exchanged greetings and then, since both women had been admiring the chapel, Kateri ventured to ask Marie Theresa,

"Where do you think the women will sit?"

"I imagine we'll be here on the right side," replied Marie Theresa.

Kateri nodded in agreement, then speaking aloud her inner thoughts, she said, "This chapel is so beautiful, and yet it is in our hearts and souls that God truly wishes to dwell."

Marie Theresa was deeply moved by Kateri's words. Did Kateri know her story?... But how could she...? They had never met before.

"Kateri, can we go to sit down over there on the big stones? There is something I wish to tell you."

There was the pain of a bitter memory in Marie Theresa's face as she began to tell her story.

"I was baptized a Christian as a young girl, but after my marriage to a non-Christian brave, I fell lax in my Faith. My husband's relatives did not approve of my religion. They encouraged me to drink firewater and partake in their pagan festivals. I did not have the courage to go against them. May God forgive me for the many sins I committed...."

Tears of sorrow filled Marie Theresa's eyes as she recalled those unhappy and foolish days of her youth. Taking a deep breath, she continued speaking.

"When my sister moved to the Laprairie settlement, I convinced my husband that we

**Kateri and Marie Theresa soon
became inseparable friends.**

should move, too. Being near other Christians made it easier for me to live my Faith, but then the urge for firewater again led to my downfall. I had been away from the sacraments for many months when it came time to leave for the winter hunt.

"We started out in the early autumn, but soon our food supply began to diminish. Then came heavy snowfalls which made hunting impossible.

"Hunger plagued us. We lived only on the bark of trees and roots. We struggled on, day after day, hardly knowing how we would be able to continue.

"My husband became very sick and died. His last words were words of regret that he had not let the Blackrobes baptize him. I felt more alone then than ever before. Yet, my main thought was not my loneliness or sorrow, but the thought that I too might die without having a chance to confess my sins. I prayed and begged Rawanniio to spare me so I could do penance for my past life of sin.

"At last, the hunters caught a wolf and his flesh sustained those of us who were left until we reached the Ottawa River. During the last days of the trip we were again without food, but it did not matter. I knew we would soon be back in Laprairie. There I found the Blackrobes. They gave us food for our weakened bodies. But what was more important, my starved soul was also nourished."

Marie Theresa's head had been down while she related her story. Now slowly she raised it so her eyes could meet Kateri's. Kateri's face was full of understanding and compassion, without a trace of scorn or shock. Kateri's shy smile gave Marie Theresa a new surge of courage and resolution.

"Marie Theresa," whispered Kateri, "God has been very good to you as He has to me. Perhaps together we can live a life of prayer and penance as a small expression of our gratitude to Him."

Kateri and Marie Theresa soon became inseparable friends. They worked together in the fields, prayed together and shared with each other the desire to spend their lives entirely for God.

One June morning, Marie Theresa came to tell Kateri some exciting news.

"Kateri, two canoes will leave today for Ville Marie (Montreal) where our deerskin blankets, wampum belts and moccasins can be sold at the white man's market. But while the others are taking care of the trading, we can visit the holy white women at the Hotel-Dieu."

Kateri quickly agreed to Marie Theresa's plan. They had often heard people talk about the holy white women who staffed the Hotel-Dieu. Father Cholenec called them "Sisters," but neither Kateri nor Marie Theresa knew much about them.

The sisters at the Hotel-Dieu greeted the two girls and gave them a tour of their hospital. Both French and Indian patients were given the same loving care. As they passed from one room to another, Marie Theresa asked their guide a number of questions. The Sisters of the Hotel-Dieu, like the Sisters of Notre Dame who staffed a school also in Montreal, had dedicated their lives entirely to God. They all dressed alike, lived together, had certain hours dedicated to prayer and made a vow of virginity.

"A vow of virginity?" Kateri's shy voice repeated the sister's last words in an attempt to fully understand their meaning.

"Yes, my dear," Sister further explained. "We do not marry so that our love and our life can be given exclusively to God. It is through this total consecration to Him that we are able to best serve our neighbor in His name."

Tears of joy welled up in Kateri's eyes. The sister's words perfectly expressed the sentiments that she had kept carefully locked in her heart. No one had understood her reason for not marrying; not even she had understood it to the fullest. But now she could dedicate herself to Jesus anew with a solemn promise, a vow that would be her marriage bond with an eternal Spouse.

Kateri's "Wedding Day"

For weeks after their return from Ville Marie, Kateri and Marie Theresa spoke of nothing else but their visit to the sisters. They were both ablaze with new ideas and plans.

"Kateri," Marie Theresa exclaimed one day, "why can't we start our own convent somewhere near the village? We could live apart from the others, praying and working as do the sisters in Ville Marie. By selling our belts and moccasins, we would have the means to help the poor and sick."

"That's a wonderful idea, Marie Theresa, but maybe we should ask a third girl to join us, someone who may know more about the life of a sister."

Marie Theresa thought for a moment and then said, "I know the perfect person—Marie

Skarichions. She's older and used to live at the Mission of Our Lady of Loretto in Quebec."

The three women met to discuss their plans. As Marie Theresa had foreseen, Marie Skarichions' acquaintance with the nuns in Quebec had left her with a practical knowledge of convent life.

"Now, all we have to decide on is where the convent should be," concluded Marie Theresa enthusiastically.

Looking across the river, her eyes fell on the Island of Herons. "Oh, there would be the perfect place," Marie Theresa exclaimed, answering her own inquiry.

Kateri had been carefully listening to every word of their conversation. An important thought suddenly came to her.

"Oh, there is one more thing we should do before we go further ahead with our plans."

"What's that, Kateri?" the other two asked.

"We want to be sure that our idea is God's will. We must tell Father Fremin all that we have discussed and accept whatever advice he gives us."

They agreed and sent Marie Theresa to Father as their representative.

Father Fremin broke into a wide smile as Marie Theresa revealed their scheme. The fervor with which she spoke touched his heart but the impracticability of such an idea turned his smile into subdued laughter.

Marie Theresa was somewhat surprised by Father's reaction. He met her questioning gaze with words spoken from paternal love.

"My dear, I'm sure our Lord is pleased with the holy desires of your soul. But the plan you have just described to me is not what He wants of you. Religious communities are not founded overnight or by those who are still new in the Faith. Be content to continue living with your families. Give them good example and pray for them. This is what God wants of you."

Marie Theresa returned to the others with her disappointing news. They accepted it as a matter of obedience and never again thought about their "convent" on Heron Island.

While Kateri and her two companions had been speaking about starting a religious community, others had been talking about an entirely different subject.

Kateri's friends, who knew nothing of her desires to belong only to Jesus, were dismayed by the fact that she was still unmarried. They were certain that the girl did not realize what hardships and difficulties would be hers if she did not marry soon.

One day while they were at home alone, one of the squaws confronted Kateri with a series of well-chosen arguments.

"Kateri, you are not getting any younger. Think of your future.... Who will support you in your older years if you do not marry now?

"I know of the ordeal you suffered when your aunt and uncle tried to trick you into a marriage with a pagan brave, but the young men of our village are all fine Christians. I know of more than one who would be pleased to have you for a wife.

"As a good Christian wife and mother, you can increase the Christian community here. We have all heard the Blackrobes speak about the beauty and holiness of Christian marriage. You are leaving yourself open to dangers if you do not marry!"

The squaw's words were like stinging bits of sand hitting against a wound that refused to close. Why did they keep insisting on marriage? Did they not see that it was impossible for her to give in to their demands?

Controlling the emotion within her, Kateri answered the squaw calmly. "Thank you for your words of counsel, but I do *not* wish to marry. I will work to support myself. I have never been afraid or ashamed of hard work."

But the squaw did not let the matter end there. She went and told Anastasia, whom she knew Kateri respected as a mother. The older woman promised to have a talk with the girl.

Anastasia's voice was stern and to the point. "Kateri, your foolish behavior is causing people to talk. It is unheard of for a Mohawk girl to remain unmarried. You must put an end to your stubbornness and obey your elders who know more than you!"

Kateri could no longer control the flow of tears that had been pushing themselves forward with each of Anastasia's piercing words. Yet there was still only one answer she could give.

"I do *not* wish to marry.... I will *not* marry.... Please do not speak to me again about this subject."

Kateri left the cabin and ran to see Father Cholenec. She must disclose her secret to him. He would understand and help her.

"Father Cholenec, may I speak with you? There is something very important that I must tell you."

Why did they keep insisting on marriage? Did they not see that it was impossible for her to give into their demands?

"I always have time to listen to my spiritual children. Come in, Kateri. How can I help you?"

"Father, some of the women will not stop talking to me about marriage. They insist that it is the course I must follow. I know they mean well...but, Father, how can I marry a man when my heart belongs to Jesus alone? I wish to dedicate my entire life to Him.... Father, may I make a vow of virginity?"

Father Cholenec was astonished at Kateri's words. What she was asking had not been requested by any Mohawk girl before her. For years he had labored among the Indians, content to see that their pagan ways were left behind when they embraced Christianity. And here before him was a young girl who on her own had gone beyond his simple instruction, aspiring to the heroic life of total consecration to God.

"My dear Kateri, how pleased our Lord must be with the generous offer of the gift you so ardently desire to give Him. Be in peace, child; you have chosen the better part and it will not be taken from you."

Kateri's face became radiant with joy. Father Cholenec set March 25, the feast of the Annunciation, as the day on which she would pronounce her vow. It was several months away, so she would have time to prepare herself for this solemn day with prayer and penance. She thanked the missionary priest and ran to share the news with her sole confidante, Marie Theresa.

No sooner had Kateri left Father Cholenec than the angry Anastasia appeared at his door. He let her vent her emotions and then said in an admonishing voice, "Truly, I am surprised that a good Christian woman like you could be so blind. Your insisting has caused Kateri considerable torment. The girl has chosen to remain a virgin because her heart belongs solely to God. It is the same life the Blessed Mother chose. Would you dare to deny her such a choice?"

His words were like a thunderbolt, striking her to the quick. Anastasia begged the priest to grant her forgiveness for the suffering she had caused Kateri.

After years of struggle, Kateri's freedom was without challengers. Her victory had been won with perseverance and iron-willed determination.

Kateri's preparation for her "wedding day" consisted in additional penances, prayers and acts of charity.

She chastised her body in order to resemble her scourged Savior; she fasted often and when she did take food, it was mixed with ashes to deaden the taste. She said her rosary as she walked barefoot in the snow, until her frozen limbs could barely move. Each morning she attended two Masses and returned to chapel in the afternoon, praying and meditating for hours.

Nor were her acts of charity any less than her penances and prayers. She carried firewood and food to the sick and elderly, took care of their fires and made sure they had fresh water. She cared for their needs with such tenderness and generosity that the Jesuit head of the mission referred to her as an "angel of charity."

Finally, on March 25, 1679, the bride was ready to meet her Bridegroom.

Father Cholenec celebrated the 8:00 Mass. Kneeling serenely in one of the front pews was Kateri. After receiving Jesus in Holy Communion, she spent a few moments in profound thanksgiving and then pronounced her vow of perpetual virginity.

"My dear Jesus, freely and willingly do I solemnly renounce the happiness of married life in order to have You alone as my Spouse.

"My Jesus, freely and willingly do I solemnly renounce the happiness of married life in order to have You alone as my Spouse."

"Holy Mother of God, present me to your divine Son. Be my Mother. I wish to always be your obedient and faithful daughter. Help me, dear Mother, help me."

It was the happiest and most beautiful day of Kateri's life. And yet in a little more than a year would come a day of even greater joy—her entrance into eternal happiness.

The Final Offering

Spring quickly turned into summer. Kateri's thin body pushed itself on through the long days of stifling heat. But the exhausting pace she had set for herself was beginning to take its toll. A high fever confined her to bed for two weeks. Her illness was so serious that many of her companions thought there was little chance of recovery.

However, she did recover and lost no time in resuming her former practices of prayer and penance. She even went so far as to secretly put prickly branches from a brier bush under her mat so that each movement caused pain and made sleep impossible. She offered this penance for the conversion of her people in the Mohawk Valley.

"Rawanniio, let me suffer so that Your great light of truth will be seen and accepted by my people. I know their sins greatly offend You, but I beg You to forgive them. Let *me* pay for their sins. Oh, my crucified Jesus, how I desire to suffer with You for the sake of their souls!"

This new penance coupled with her already weak health left her in a state of total exhaustion. Her close friend, Marie Theresa, who had joined Kateri in so many other practices of penance, was frightened by Kateri's condition.

"Kateri," Marie Theresa said with notable concern, "I cannot help but see how weak you are. You are hardly able to walk. What are you doing to yourself? I know it must be some new penance. Tell me, Kateri. We have never kept secrets from each other."

Kateri pulled back the covers of her mat and revealed the thorn branches that were responsible for her sleepless nights.

"But, Kateri," protested Marie Theresa, "our Lord does not want you to kill yourself. Besides, such extreme penances cannot be undertaken without the permission of your confessor."

Marie Theresa's words startled her. The thought that she might be doing something wrong had never entered her mind. She immediately ran to confess her "sin" to Father Cholenec. Her words filled the priest with admiration, but he knew it was his duty to reprimand her for such imprudence.

"Kateri," he said sternly, "you are to go back to your cabin and throw those branches in the fire. You are too weak to even consider such a penance!"

"Yes, Father, I will do as you say at once."

As he watched her walk away, Father Cholenec could not help but reflect on Kateri's profound spirit of docility. The will of God was supreme in her life; the secret of the saints had become her own.

It was March of 1680. Kateri's emaciated body lay still on her mat. The slightest movement caused her pain. She was racked with constant headaches and fever, yet her days were spent praying, especially the rosary. The crucifix was often in her hands, and she drew great consolation by meditating on the passion of Christ.

Each day the Fathers of the mission would take turns visiting her. Father Chauchetiere often brought several children with him on his visits. He taught them their catechism lessons as Kateri listened in. This pleasant diversion was most welcome to the dying girl. She who had renounced children of her own felt spiritually united to the innocent souls who gathered around her bedside to drink in the Blackrobe's stories of the Great Rawanniio.

On Palm Sunday of Holy Week, Kateri took a turn for the worse. It was evident to the Fathers that the end was near. Two members of the Holy Family Confraternity were assigned to take turns keeping a day-and-night vigil by her side.

Father Cholenec came to visit her on Monday. "Father," she whispered, "it is Holy Week. I must perform some act of penance in honor of our Lord's passion. Perhaps I can fast from food for a day?"

"No, no, Kateri," answered the priest. "The offering of your suffering is enough. Our Lord knows that you would do more if you could, and He is pleased with your holy desires. Rest now and tomorrow I will bring Jesus to you."

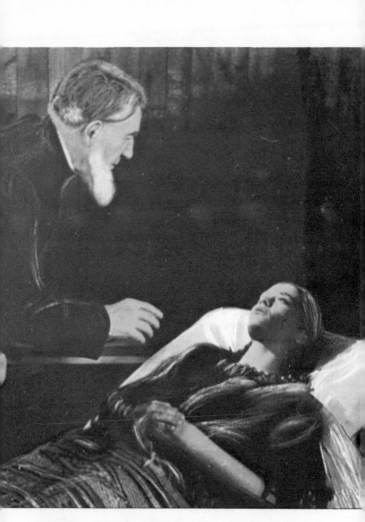

"Father," she whispered, "it is Holy Week. I must perform some act of penance in honor of our Lord's passion."

The priest's promise to bring her Holy Communion was not the ordinary procedure which was followed at the mission. Normally, the sick person was carried to the Church on a bark stretcher and received Holy Communion there. The unusual exception was made for Kateri both because of her weak condition and her exemplary life.

Kateri was alone with her friend, Marie Theresa. "Marie Theresa," Kateri said in a worried voice, "I am not dressed properly to receive our Lord. I gave all my clothes away to the poor since I knew I would no longer need them. But now...."

"Don't worry, Kateri," reassured Marie Theresa in a soothing voice, "I will take care of you." And in a few moments she returned with her own Sunday dress which she put on Kateri.

A short time later, Father Cholenec arrived with the Blessed Sacrament. He was followed by a crowd of villagers who had spontaneously formed a procession behind him.

Kateri knew it was her last meeting with Jesus on this earth. Her thanksgiving was one of profound gratitude to the God who had blessed her with such abundant graces.

The Indians who had gathered inside and outside of her cabin now began to file past her one by one. "Do not forget us, little sister. Tell Rawanniio of our needs. He will listen to you."

Kateri, who had always been shy and reserved, was still able to find the right words for each person. "Yes, I will pray for you.... Pray for my poor soul, too.... Be strong in our beautiful Faith.... Love Jesus.... Love Mary...."

The next day, Wednesday, April 17, 1680, the twenty-four-year-old maiden was anointed. At 3:00 in the afternoon, her last agony began. The priests and Indians who had gathered around her mat prayed together aloud. Her breaths grew shorter and shorter. "Jesus! Mary! I love you," were her last whispered words before she quietly slept in the arms of her eternal Bridegroom.

Neither the priests nor the faithful present moved from the room. They remained in silent prayer and thus merited to witness first-hand the sign of God's predilection for the Mohawk maiden. Father Cholenec, who was kneeling next to her, suddenly cried out in astonishment, "Look, her face, her face.... The scars are gone!"

**"Be strong in our beautiful Faith....
Love Jesus.... Love Mary...."**

Her skin, which had been disfigured by smallpox scars and illness, was now smooth and beautiful. The radiant beauty of her soul, which had always been visible to God, was now evident to all in the bright glow which lit up her peaceful face.

Epilogue

Devotion to the "Lily of the Mohawks" became widespread among both the Indian and French population. In 1715, Father Cholenec wrote to his Provincial in France: "All the French who live in these colonies—as well as the Indians—have a singular devotion to her. They come from afar to pray at her tomb; several have been cured of illnesses through her intercession, and have received from heaven other wonderful favors."

In 1744, in his *History and Description of New France,* Father de Charlevoix, S.J., told his readers that this young Mohawk woman was then "...universally considered as the protectress of Canada and as the 'new star of the New World.'"

"Happy the poor in spirit! Happy the meek! Happy the pure of heart!"

The Third Plenary Council of Baltimore in 1884 petitioned the Holy See to institute the process for the beatification of Kateri Tekakwitha.

On May 22, 1931, the cause was instituted by the Most Reverend Bishop of Albany, Edmund F. Gibbons. The process was finished on June 4, 1932. On May 20, 1939, His Holiness, Pope Pius XII, approved the introduction of Kateri's cause and on January 3, 1943, the same Pope issued the decree of heroicity. His Holiness offered the holy Sacrifice of the Mass and then solemnly proclaimed: "It has been proved in this instance and for the purpose under consideration, that the theological virtues of faith, hope, love of God and neighbor, and the cardinal virtues of prudence, justice, temperance, fortitude and subordinate virtues of the Venerable Servant of God, Kateri Tekakwitha, were heroic."

And on June 22, 1980, at the Basilica of St. Peter in Rome, Pope John Paul II declared her Blessed Kateri Tekakwitha.

Blessed Kateri Tekakwitha left this earth 300 years ago. But her message for today's world, where morals, materialism and violence run rampant, is the same message she gave her own people: What peace and freedom the children of God possess! Happy the poor in spirit! Happy the meek! Happy the pure of heart!

Blessed
Kateri Tekakwitha

Lily of the Mohawks

Born at Auriesville, NY, 1656
Baptized at Fonda, NY, 1676
Died at Caughnawaga, Canada,
April 17, 1680
Declared Venerable by Pope Pius XII
January 3, 1943
Beatified by Pope John Paul II
June 22, 1980

O God, who, among the many marvels of Your grace in the New World, did cause to blossom on the banks of the Mohawk and of the St. Lawrence, the pure and tender Lily, Kateri Tekakwitha, grant, we beseech You, the favor we beg through her intercession—that this young lover of Jesus and of His cross may soon be counted among her saints by Holy Mother Church, and that our hearts may be enkindled with a stronger desire to imitate her innocence and faith. Through the same Christ our Lord. Amen.

Imprimatur:
+ Most Reverend Howard J. Hubbard, D.D.

Daughters of St. Paul

IN MASSACHUSETTS
  50 St. Paul's Ave. Jamaica Plain, Boston, MA 02130;
    617-522-8911; 617-522-0875;
  172 Tremont Street, Boston, MA 02111; **617-426-5464;**
    617-426-4230
IN NEW YORK
  78 Fort Place, Staten Island, NY 10301; **212-447-5071**
  59 East 43rd Street, New York, NY 10017; **212-986-7580**
  7 State Street, New York, NY 10004; **212-447-5071**
  625 East 187th Street, Bronx, NY 10458; **212-584-0440**
  525 Main Street, Buffalo, NY 14203; **716-847-6044**
IN NEW JERSEY
  Hudson Mall — Route 440 and Communipaw Ave.,
    Jersey City, NJ 07304; **201-433-7740**
IN CONNECTICUT
  202 Fairfield Ave., Bridgeport, CT 06604; **203-335-9913**
IN OHIO
  2105 Ontario St. (at Prospect Ave.), Cleveland, OH 44115; **216-621-9427**
  25 E. Eighth Street, Cincinnati, OH 45202; **513-721-4838**
IN PENNSYLVANIA
  1719 Chestnut Street, Philadelphia, PA 19103; **215-568-2638**
IN FLORIDA
  2700 Biscayne Blvd., Miami, FL 33137; **305-573-1618**
IN LOUISIANA
  4403 Veterans Memorial Blvd., Metairie, LA 70002; **504-887-7631;**
    504-887-0113
  1800 South Acadian Thruway, P.O. Box 2028, Baton Rouge, LA 70821
    504-343-4057; 504-343-3814
IN MISSOURI
  1001 Pine Street (at North 10th), St. Louis, MO 63101; **314-621-0346;**
    314-231-5522
IN ILLINOIS
  172 North Michigan Ave., Chicago, IL 60601; **312-346-4228**
IN TEXAS
  114 Main Plaza, San Antonio, TX 78205; **512-224-8101**
IN CALIFORNIA
  1570 Fifth Avenue, San Diego, CA 92101; **714-232-1442**
  46 Geary Street, San Francisco, CA 94108; **415-781-5180**
IN HAWAII
  1143 Bishop Street, Honolulu, HI 96813; **808-521-2731**
IN ALASKA
  750 West 5th Avenue, Anchorage AK 99501; **907-272-8183**
IN CANADA
  3022 Dufferin Street, Toronto 395, Ontario, Canada
IN ENGLAND
  57, Kensington Church Street, London W. 8, England
IN AUSTRALIA
  58 Abbotsford Rd., Homebush, N.S.W., Sydney 2140, Australia